RoadkillRecipes

AUSTRALIAN WILDLIFE ON THE VERGE

Patricia and Tim Leeuwenburg

Leeuwenburg, Patricia.
Roadkill recipes: Australian wildlife on the verge.

ISBN 9780975848319.

1. Roadkill-Australia 2. Cookery, Australian-Humor 3. Traffic safety and wildlife-Australia
4. Wildlife conservation-Australia
Leeuwenburg, Tim. II. Title.

641.690207

Contents

About the Authors

The roadkill phenomenon first interested Patricia and Tim during their travels within Australia. Every roadkill encounter brought with it many questions and long discussions that continue to this day.

Patricia's interest in wildlife and the pressures of tourism and development in regional areas led her to undertake research on the abundant roadkill of Kangaroo Island, South Australia.

As a local doctor on Kangaroo Island, Tim has a vested interest in reducing human injury from wildlife-vehicle collisions. His research in this area won the prize for best paper at 'Trauma 2007', the Australasian Trauma Society annual meeting.

Together they published 'Roadkill Recipes: A Cookbook for Visitors to Kangaroo Island' in January 2006. The book was a success with both visitors and locals alike. The book highlights the confronting issue of roadkill, emphasising important conservation and road safety messages whilst satirising glossy cookbooks and gourmet travel.

'Roadkill Recipes: Australian Wildlife on the Verge' takes the theme a step further, portraying an overview of Australian roadkill with a twist for the gallivanting gourmet.

Bon appetit!

Leeuwenburg, P (2004) 'Roadkill on Kangaroo Island: Identification of patterns and predictors of roadkill' Honours Thesis B. Appl. Sci. (Biodiversity, Environment & Park Management) University of South Australia.

Leeuwenburg, T (2007) 'Recipes from disaster: a novel approach to reducing wildlife-vehicle collisions on Kangaroo Island, South Australia' Paper presented at Australasian Trauma Society Meeting 13-14th October 2007, Melbourne, Victoria.

DISCLAIMER

The authors emphasise that NO ANIMALS were harmed specifically for the making of this book. These recipes are intended as satire only. We do not condone roadkill, nor the removal and preparation of native animals using the recipes herein.

Native animals are protected in many States. Killing (and/or removal) of native wildlife without appropriate permits is illegal and may attract severe penalties.

Roadkill Recipes - Wildlife on the Verge

There is increasing awareness of roadkill as an important conservation issue. The dual meaning of the title was chosen as a reminder that wherever roads encroach into wildlife habitat there will be wildlife: both on the verge of the road and in some cases on the verge of extinction.

Wildlife use both the road and verge environment as transport corridors and as an easy, often preferable resource area. Unfortunately the indiscriminate, contemporary predator of this environment, the car or truck, can place vulnerable species or populations on the verge of extinction.

Many native Australian species are already stressed from habitat loss, predation and disease. For those species, the added pressures of roadkill really can lead to wildlife populations existing 'on the verge'.

Whilst 'Roadkill Recipes' may attract some criticism, we believe satirical humour is justified to raise awareness. On the roadkill 'hotspot' of Kangaroo Island, our first book succeeded in this regard. Part-profits from book sales are used to fund a 'Watch Out for Wildlife' car-sticker campaign.

We believe that bringing the subject of roadkill to a broader audience will encourage debate and build greater awareness of what to expect on the road, serving both road safety and wildlife conservation efforts.

What brings wildlife to the verge?

animal behaviour
eg: young dispersing to new territory, reptiles basking on bitumen, animals crossing to access water or pasture; carrion feeders such as goannas, Tasmanian devils & raptors feeding on roadkill

roadside topography
eg: presence of water in roadside culverts or streams may attract animals to drink; drainage may encourage herbaceous plant growth, attractive to grazers

Counting Roadkill

Roadkill is well known to anyone who has driven in rural Australia. For some people it may be their only encounter with native wildlife. Unfortunately wherever human transportation networks and wildlife coincide one can expect to find roadkill.

Variables determining roadkill are extensive but include:
- wildlife density and behaviour
- time of year
- traffic density and speed
- roadside features

Accurate counts of roadkill are difficult to determine. Definitive statistics are lacking, with any counts likely to be an underestimate as carcasses counted on the road or verge represent only a fraction of animals killed by vehicles. Try counting roadkill for yourself on a long country drive.

In Tasmania, a report from RACT Insurance in 2008 describes 8 successive years of growth in the number of claims from motorists who have hit an animal, or swerved to avoid one. The average cost of repairs was more than $4,700 per collision.

ABC News Feb 9, 2008
http://abc.net.au/news/stories/2008/02/09/2158518.htm

Sources such as the NSW Wildlife Information Rescue & Education Service (WIRES) quote 7000 native animals killed per day on NSW roads alone; researcher Alistair Hobday estimates one dead animal per 2.7 km of road in Tasmania, concentrated in 'hotspots'; the data from Kangaroo Island suggests an average of one dead animal per 3.6 km per day, again concentrated in 'hotspots'.

Many collisions involving wildlife are not reported; even crashes resulting in human injury requiring hospital treatment may not be coded as involving wildlife (especially where drivers lose control and hit a fixed object such as a tree after swerving to avoid a collision). Data from motor vehicle insurers (who have a vested interest in reducing human and vehicle damage) suggest that wildlife - vehicle collisions are on the increase. NRMA statistics suggest a national repair bill of $21 million in 2006 and an estimated overall national community cost of $70 million for the consequences of such collisions in Australia each year.

Rules of the Road

Not only is roadkill readily available for free, the meat is mostly lean and low GI.

Fresh meat is always the rule

(If it's still on the road on the way home, it's too late)

Semi-squashed is much better than squashed

(anything clobbered by a road train is probably undesirable)

Sealed roads are preferred over dirt roads

(Digging gravel out of your meal can be a chore)

Animal rights group PETA (People for the Ethical Treatment of Animals) ran a campaign entitled 'Roadkill – meat without the murder', highlighting the fact that "roadkill is natural, organic, and pesticide-free!" www.peta.org/feat/roadkill

Ethical issues aside, we hope that 'Roadkill Recipes' will, through a touch of humour, help to make you smile and think about the road you're on.

Tasty Treats

A gentle introduction to roadkill cuisine; these dishes can be prepared in isolation as a roadside snack or enjoyed as part of a wider degustation menu experience.

Splatter Bug Dip

Echidna Shashliks

Sautéed Cane Toad Legs

Possum Pizza

Splatter Bug Dip

INGREDIENTS

1 cup assorted insects
2 tsp milk
2 cups cottage cheese
3 tbs mayonnaise
1 small onion, finely chopped
1 tsp butter
1/4 cup parsley, chopped
1 tsp black pepper

METHOD

Using a mortar and pestle (or a rock and a hard place) crush insects scraped from windscreen, headlights etc.

Heat butter and sauté crushed insects with pepper and onion. Allow to cool. Meanwhile combine all other ingredients and mix to a soft paste. Add cooled, sautéed insects, mix well. Chill or serve immediately with corn chips or water crackers if hungry.

Chef's Tip
According to the experts, insects can quickly become unpalatable after death. Unless you can stop continuously to clean and freeze your front grill 'catch', the preferred method is to only make dip immediately after driving through a swarm of insects.

Echidna Shashliks

INGREDIENTS

200g echidna meat, diced
32 echidna spines
4 cloves garlic, crushed
4 tbs white wine vinegar
2 tbs lemon juice
1tsp ground black pepper
1 white onion, grated
1/2 cup parsley, finely chopped
8 lemon wedges

Serves 4

METHOD

Combine white wine vinegar, lemon juice, garlic, grated onion, pepper and parsley in a bowl to marinate echidna cubes overnight. Prepare spines by washing then coat with oil. Push meat onto spines alternating with onion pieces and capsicum. Douse with olive oil and grill on barbeque or hot plate.

Serve immediately with lemon wedges, tabouli salad and your choice of spicy native berry or cucumber sauces.

Chef's Tip
As an alternative try 'Gypsy-style Echidna Baked in Clay' from Roadkill Recipes: a Cookbook for Visitors to Kangaroo Island.

Sautéed Cane Toad Legs

INGREDIENTS

8 pairs cane toad legs
1 cup flour
1/2 tsp each paprika, thyme
1 pinch salt
1 tsp cracked black pepper
50g butter
2 cloves garlic, minced
1/2 cup tomato, diced
1/2 cup spring onions, chopped
1 red capsicum, sliced
dash dry white wine
parsley & lemon for garnish

Serves 4

METHOD

Carefully remove skin from toad legs, rinse in water & pat dry with paper towel. Combine paprika, salt, cracked pepper and thyme with flour. Dredge toad legs in seasoned flour, shake to remove excess and set aside. Melt butter in heated pan. Add legs and sauté until golden. Add garlic and spring onion; continue to sauté for 1 minute. Add tomato, capsicum and a dash of dry white wine. Simmer for 2 minutes. Remove from heat. Serve with parsley and a slice of lemon.

Chef's Tip
Keep your eyes open...the largest reported cane toad was 2.65 kg - enough to feed a family! Seriously though, despite being an environmental invader, cane toads are toxic - do NOT eat them.

Bufotenin, a chemical excreted by the cane toad, is reputed to have psychoactive effects similar to LSD and mescaline. The cane toad excretes bufotenin in very small amounts at the same time as excreting other more lethal toxins in relatively large amounts on their skin; hence toad licking for the potential mild hallucinogenic effect of bufotenin is likely to result in serious illness or death.

Resist the temptation to lick or eat a cane toad!

Possum Pizza

INGREDIENTS

100g possum meat, finely sliced
1 x 25 cm pizza base
1 tsp olive oil
2 tbs tomato paste
2 medium tomatoes, sliced
3 sprigs curly leaf parsley, torn
8 stuffed green olives, sliced
1/2 onion, finely sliced
1 clove garlic, chopped
1/4 cup mozzarella cheese
1/4 cup matured cheddar cheese

Serves 2

METHOD

Preheat oven. Heat oil in small pan and toss possum slices until they begin to change colour. Set aside. Cover pizza base with tomato paste. Add garlic and tomato slices. Top with onion, possum slices and olives.

Mix the two cheeses together then sprinkle over the pizza. Use more or less cheese according to taste. Cook in oven for 15 - 20 minutes, sprinkle with parsley and serve with sliced grape tomatoes.

ROPE BRIDGES

Roads present a barrier for many species. Rope bridges allow arboreal species such as possums an opportunity to cross roads without having to leave the safety of the tree canopy.

Main Courses

Skippy the Bush Vindaloo

Wombat Fillet à la Freycinet

Coastal Koala Stack

Shabu Shabu Bandicoot

Parma Wallaby

Roadkill Meat Pie

Don't be afraid to experiment. Use the handy conversion table below as a rough guide. Smaller species are best served as delicious entrees, saving the larger ones for main course.

NUMBER	SPECIES
1	Kangaroo
2	Wallaroos or Wombats
4	Wallabies or Koalas
6	Tasmanian Devils or Echidnas
8	Pademelons or Spotted-tailed Quolls
12 - 20	Quokkas or Brushtail Possums
30+	Potoroos, Bilbies, Southern Brown Bandicoots, or Numbats
>50	Fat-tailed Dunnarts, Eastern Pygmy Possums or Antechinus

Ideal for cookery in the outback - nothing beats a hearty meal under the wide Australian skies at night.

Skippy the Bush Vindaloo

INGREDIENTS

800g kangaroo, cubed
3 potatoes, diced
2 brown onions, finely sliced
2 dried red chilli peppers
1 tbs cracked black pepper
1 tsp fennel seed, crushed
1 tsp cumin seed, crushed
5 tbs white wine vinegar
1 tbs fine brown sugar
1 tbs crushed garlic
2 tbs ginger, finely chopped
2 tbs vegetable oil
1 tsp salt

Raita

1 cucumber, finely diced
2 cups low fat plain yoghurt
pinch each coriander, cumin

Serves 4

METHOD

Heat a dash of oil and quickly dry fry chilli, black pepper, cumin and fennel. Remove from heat and grind spices together. Add salt, sugar and 1/2 of the vinegar. Mix and let stand. Heat oil in large heavy based pot. Add onions, stirring regularly until golden brown. Remove onions from pot and puree with 1 tbs water. Combine onion puree with vinegar and spice mix to form a paste.

Heat garlic and ginger in remaining oil. Add roo cubes a handful at a time to seal on all sides (removing each time). When finished, heat spice paste in pot. Return all meat to pot and add potatoes as mix becomes aromatic. Add 1/3 cup of water and boil for 2 minutes then slow cook for up to 1 hour. Add water and remainder of vinegar to taste. Serve with rice and raita.

Wombat Fillet à la Freycinet

INGREDIENTS

2 wombat fillets
2 tsp olive oil
1 tsp lemon juice
1/2 tsp crushed garlic
sea salt and peppercorns, crushed
snow pea shoots
green salad leaves
4 mini gourmet deli-style hot peppers pre-stuffed with feta cheese
Tasmanian plum and pepperberry sauce

Serves 2

METHOD

Combine lemon juice, garlic, oil, salt and pepper in a large bowl.
Add tenderised wombat fillets and stand for at least 30 minutes.
Take out the camp stove and fire up the gas.

Arrange the wombat fillets on a green base of shoots and leaves.
Add stuffed peppers. Drizzle fillets with native Tasmanian plum
and pepperberry sauce. Garnish with snow pea shoots.

Chef's Tip
This simple recipe can be adapted for any type of wombat - Northern, Southern, Hairy or otherwise.
We found ours at Tasmania's stunning Freycinet Peninsula.

Coastal Koala Stack

INGREDIENTS

1 coastal koala
3 cloves garlic, crushed
1/2 cup olive oil
2 cups white wine
2 tbs coastal eucalypt honey
freshly ground black pepper
8 slices pumpkin
2 red capsicums, sliced
8 fingers aubergine
baby spinach leaves
rosemary garnish

Serves 4

METHOD

Slice meat into 8 palm-sized fillets each approximately 1cm thick. Combine garlic, oil, wine, honey and pepper in shallow dish. Add meat and marinate for 2 hours. Char grill aubergine, pumpkin and capsicum pieces. Keep warm. Heat ribbed skillet. Cook marinated fillets 2-3 minutes on each side over high heat. Blanche spinach for 30 seconds. Arrange on plates stacked with pumpkin, aubergine and spinach topped with capsicum and rosemary garnish. Serve immediately with a crisp white wine of your choice.

In Queensland, roadkill accounts for around 30% of koala deaths along the 375 sq. km 'Koala Coast' region. Many of these koalas are young healthy males. Their loss compounds the impact on overall population viability by removing otherwise healthy individuals.   Dique et al. (2003)

Chef's Tip 1
Be sure to check your koala for Chlamydia before cooking.

Chef's Tip 2
There is no need to add salt as the coastal environment has imbued your koala with delicious natural sea salts. Use honey from the coastal eucalypt flower to enhance the freshness of the meat's distinctive eucalypt flavour.

Shabu Shabu Bandicoot

INGREDIENTS

400g bandicoot, thinly sliced
1 tbs vegetable oil
4 tbs ginger, ground
1 tbs ginger, chopped
2 cloves garlic, crushed
1/2 cup soy sauce
2 cups vegetable stock
1 tsp castor sugar
1/2 Chinese cabbage, finely sliced
2 spring onions, sliced
1 medium red capsicum, sliced
cracked pepper to taste

Serves 4

METHOD

Heat vegetable oil in pan. Sauté garlic and chopped ginger until golden brown. Add soy sauce and 1/4 cup vegetable stock. Remove from heat and stir in sugar, then reduce mixture over low heat. Strain and set aside. Cook cabbage until translucent in salted boiling water. Drain and arrange on plate. Bring remaining vegetable stock and ground ginger to a gentle boil. Dip each bandicoot slice in and out of the stock, moving in a left to right motion and back, poaching until medium-rare. Arrange on top of the cabbage, topping with capsicum and spring onion slivers. Reheat sauce; drizzle over bandicoot meat, then sprinkle with cracked pepper. Serve immediately.

Chef's Tip
Shabu shabu loosely equates to what some might described as a Japanese hot pot. However, the exquisite nature of the experience is definitely lost in such a translation! It is the art of swishing a delicately thin slice of meat through ginger stock (dashi). Let your guests try it for themselves. Speaking out aloud, swish one way "shabu" then swish back "shabu"...a nice fluid movement "shabu shabu".

Parma Wallaby

INGREDIENTS

4 wallaby fillets
1/2 cup breadcrumbs
6 tbs Parmesan cheese, grated
1/4 cup plain flour
2 eggs
1 tbs olive oil
2 x 400g can crushed tomatoes
2 tsp garlic, crushed
1 tsp each dried oregano, basil
1 fist mozzarella cheese, shredded
100g fettuccine
2 tbs butter
4 sprigs fresh basil, chopped
2 tsp mint, chopped
2 tsp black pepper, cracked

Serves 4

Chef's Tip
One of the problems encountered with roadside cookery is that you can't always find the exact ingredients when or where you need them. Using the conversion table on page 12 should help to ease stress when trying to prepare a little something special whilst on the road.

METHOD

Combine breadcrumbs, 3 tbs Parmesan, salt, pepper and oregano. Coat wallaby fillet with flour, dip in beaten egg, then coat in seasoned crumb mix. Heat oil in a skillet and cook wallaby each side until brown. Set aside. Combine garlic, crushed tomatoes and dried basil over medium heat. Simmer until mixture begins to thicken. Cover the base of a dish in tomato mixture. Arrange crumbed wallaby fillets on top. Cover with remaining tomato mixture. Place shredded mozzarella on top of fillets, cover and bake for 30 minutes. Uncover, top with remaining Parmesan and bake for a further 10 minutes. Cook pasta then toss with butter, cracked pepper and fresh mint. Serve wallaby nestled safely between two bushes of fresh pepper and mint pasta.

Roadkill Meat Pie

INGREDIENTS

300g assorted roadkill meats, diced and minced
2 tbs each flour, olive oil
3 cloves garlic, chopped
1 onion, finely chopped
1 tbs each black pepper, coriander
1 cup tomato sauce
1/8 cup Worcestershire sauce
1/4 cup soy sauce
4 cups roadkill stock
2 sheets puff pastry
1 egg yolk

Serves 2 adults or one small dog

METHOD

Preheat camp oven to very hot. Fry onions in hot oil until clear. Add garlic and assorted meats stirring until browned. Add remaining spices, tomato, soy and Worcestershire sauces. Reduce liquid then add stock. Simmer until meat begins to break apart. Mix flour and water to form a paste. Gradually add stock to thin out paste and pour into meat mix, stirring constantly until thickened. Season to taste. Cool. Grease pie dishes. Spoon in cooled meat mixture. Cover with puff pastry. Seal and finish edges with a fork. Glaze with beaten egg yolk. Cook in camp oven till golden. Serve fresh with a garden salad.

Chef's Tip
If it doesn't taste as good as you thought, then the dog won't mind!

Birds of a Feather

A light and feathery selection of birds that like to keep their feet on the ground.

Leg O'Mu

Baked Mallee Fowl Mound

Curlew Croquettes on a Bush Stone

Cassowary Rollover

Leg O'Mu

INGREDIENTS

1 emu leg
2 cloves garlic, crushed
1 tbs each salt, pepper
2 tbs each parsley, thyme, chopped
1 tbs coriander paste
1/2 cup olive oil
1 tbs each gin, mirin
2 tbs soy sauce
1 bottle red wine

Serves 2

METHOD

Combine salt, pepper, garlic and herbs with oil, mirin, gin and
soy. Remove bony part of leg (or it won't fit in the camp oven!).
Rub herb marinade over meat, place in a camp oven, pour in
excess marinade, cover and leave for 2 hours. Place camp oven
on hot coals (or on hot engine). Add some red wine and cook
until tender. Toss in some potatoes, carrots and white onions at
about the halfway mark.

Don't forget to check wine levels regularly; try not to let yourself
or the roast dry out!

Chef's Tip
Be careful not to overcook your emu. Emu meat has a very low fat content.

Baked Mallee Fowl Mound

INGREDIENTS

4 pieces of mallee fowl
2 cloves garlic, crushed
1 tbs thyme, chopped
2 tsp Japanese rice wine
1 tbs lime juice
2 tsp sesame oil
1 red chilli, finely sliced
8 tbs muntrie jam
zest of 1 lime
2 tbs water

Serves 4

METHOD

Mix together garlic, thyme, rice wine, chilli, lime juice and sesame oil. Place in a large bowl with mallee fowl pieces and stir together until pieces are well coated. Allow to sit for 1-2 hours in the shade. Place mallee fowl pieces on rack in a baking dish. Sprinkle generously with dried thyme and bake for 30-35 mins at moderate heat. Remove from oven, cover and let stand for 5 minutes. Gently heat muntrie jam in a small pan with water and lime zest. Serve on a mound of mash, drizzled with muntrie sauce and a side serve of steamed greens.

The nesting mound is kept at a constant 33°C. It averages a base circumference of 5 - 6 m and up to 1 m in height.

The mallee fowl is an opportunistic feeder, often foraging on and around roads, where it collects spilt grain. This behaviour makes the mallee fowl extremely susceptible to collisions with vehicles.

Curlew Croquettes on a Bush Stone

INGREDIENTS

2 bush stone curlews
40g butter
1/2 tbs oil (plus oil for deep-frying)
1/4 cup white wine, dry
1 onion, finely chopped
1 pinch nutmeg
1/4 cup parsley, finely chopped
1/2 tsp thyme
1 cup chicken stock
20g plain flour
2 eggs, separated
2 cups fine breadcrumbs

Serves 2 - 3

Bush stone curlews are dry-land predators of small grassland animals. When disturbed they 'freeze' in position like stone statues - this strategy works well against visual predators such as raptors and humans, but is ineffective against scent-based predators such as foxes.

METHOD

Pre-cook curlew meat in a pan with a dash of butter, salt, pepper and a splash of wine. Remove, cool and then chop or shred very finely. Melt butter over low heat. Add onion, herbs and spices cooking gently until onion becomes clear. Add flour stirring constantly then gradually add stock and white wine to form a smooth sauce. Remove from heat, add egg yolks and chopped curlew meat. Mix well and season to taste. Set aside to cool.

Lightly beat egg whites and place in shallow dish. Separate cold curlew mixture into 20 mm by 60 mm portions. Shape nicely then roll in breadcrumbs, dip through egg whites then roll in breadcrumbs again for a thick coat. Deep-fry a few at a time until golden. Drain on paper towel then serve on heated stones with your favourite mustard (not bustard).

INGREDIENTS

4 small cassowary fillets
1 tbs olive oil
1 tsp each cumin, paprika
1 tsp ground black pepper
1/2 cup plain yoghurt
1 mango, peeled, cut into thick slices
4 slices of Camembert cheese
mango chutney

Salad & Dressing

fresh baby rocket
1/2 Spanish onion
4 cherry tomatoes, halved
1 each mango, avocado, pieces
2 kiwi fruit, sliced
1tsp oil
1 lime, juiced

Serves 4

METHOD

Mix yoghurt, paprika, cumin and pepper in a bowl. Coat fillets thoroughly in yoghurt mix. Keep cool for at least 1 hour then layer mango and Camembert slices across the opened fillets. Rollover carefully ensuring the stuffing remains inside the roll. Secure with a stick.

Place roll on preheated hotplate and brown the outside quickly. Remove and place in a baking dish in a moderate oven for about 8 – 10 minutes. Remove from oven and let stand for 2 minutes. Serve with a healthy tropical salad and a dash of mango chutney.

The southern cassowary has a major ecological role in seed dispersal in Queensland's tropical rainforests. With a limited range restricted to remnant patches of forest, habitat fragmentation and roadkill have been identified as serious threats to the cassowary.

Splash and a Dash

How does an aquatic animal end up as roadkill?

Penguins and platypus are lithe in the water but slow and clumsy when they leave it. Some penguins cross roads to reach their nests and platypus may simply need to get to the water on the other side of a road. Other marine animals may be unlucky enough to be hit by boats.

Tuna-friendly Dolphin Sushi

Penguin Pinwheels

Platypus Poison Platter

Tuna-friendly Dolphin Sushi

INGREDIENTS

100g dolphin cuts
(no tuna by-catch)
1 cucumber, sliced
1 red capsicum
wasabi (or mayonnaise)
6 nori (seaweed) sheets
2 cups short grained rice
2 tbs rice wine vinegar
1 pinch salt
4 tsp white sugar

Serves 2 - 4

'Boatstrike' is increasingly recognised as causing injury or death to marine animals in Australia. Species affected include dugong, dolphin, whale and turtle. Surfacing to breathe and foraging in shallow waters places these animals at risk from water traffic. The innovative 'Go Slow For Those Below' campaign in Queensland aims to educate water users and reduce the incidence of boatstrike.

METHOD

Wash and cook rice. Place vinegar, sugar and salt in a small pan. Heat gently and stir to dissolve sugar. Allow to cool. Place freshly cooked rice into a large bowl. Sprinkle with cold vinegar mix and quickly but gently fold rice with a wooden spoon. Lay a nori sheet on a bamboo rolling mat. Moisten hands, take a handful of cooled rice and spread over nori. Add wasabi along centre line to taste. Add thin slices of dolphin and cucumber (or capsicum) on top of wasabi. Lift the end of the mat and roll over the ingredients with a firm gentle pressure until nori roll is complete. Slice the roll into bite sized pieces. Serve with pickled ginger, wasabi and a dash of soy sauce.

Penguin Pinwheels

INGREDIENTS

3 - 4 penguins, minced
1 clove garlic, crushed
1 tsp Worcestershire sauce
2 tbs breadcrumbs
1 brown onion, finely chopped
1 egg
100g parsley, finely chopped
2 puff pastry sheets
pinch salt & pepper seasoning

Serves 4

METHOD

Mix minced penguin meat together with onion, garlic, salt, pepper, egg, breadcrumbs and Worcestershire sauce. Add chopped parsley, mix then set aside. Take a sheet of pastry, add a handful of penguin mince and roll carefully, to form a 'pinwheel' roll of penguin ensconced in pastry.

Cut into 2 cm wide segments and baste exposed pastry. Bake for 25 minutes at medium heat until golden brown. Serve hot with sliced pumpkin, a bundle of asparagus and a dash of mustard seed whole egg mayonnaise.

Platypus Poison Platter

INGREDIENTS

1 male platypus roadkill (rare)
cheeses, cucumber, salami, olives, pineapple,
water crackers

Serves 2

METHOD

Find the 15 mm curved spur on the inside of the ankle, then carefully dissect all the way up the rear leg of your roadkill platypus to reveal the kidney-shaped venom gland on the inner thigh. Quickly fry the venom spur and apparatus for 30 seconds; set aside and allow to cool.

Meanwhile, prepare a platter of cheese, assorted meats, and refreshing pineapple & cucumber slices. Using cocktail sticks (or roadkill echidna spines) spear a selection and swallow with a dash of your favourite spirit.

NEXT
.5 km

This is reputed to be the only platypus road sign in Australia.

Chef's Tip
Warning: the venom gland attached to the spur should be swallowed whole. If chewed, accidental envenomation of the inner cheek or tongue is a real possibility. Platypus venom causes intense swelling and pain. Proximity to a well-equipped hospital is recommended before serving.

Creatures of Habit

Carrion - the decaying remains of a dead animal. This doesn't sound like the sort of thing good recipes are made of, but it can be an irresistible, energy conserving feast or at the very least a palatable alternative to no food at all.

Goanna Stir-fry

Roadside Wedgies

Quoll au Vent

Tasmanian Kidney Deville

Roadkill provides an easy food source for opportunistic scavengers but it can be a risky strategy. Attracted onto the road by a tasty roadkill meal, the scavenger may die under the wheels of passing traffic...and so on it goes.

- A goanna with its head buried in a carcass is not alert to traffic and can be difficult to see.
- Tasmanian devils and quolls feed on roadkill carcasses at night and can be difficult to see in the dark.
- Wedge-tailed eagles are very large birds that need space to take off, often flying across the road into the path of traffic.
- Feral cats are also a common secondary roadkill species.

Goanna Stir-fry

INGREDIENTS

400g goanna, skinned and chopped
200g white noodles
1/2 tsp salt
1/2 tsp mixed pepper spice
1 tbs olive oil
1 tsp sesame oil
1 red capsicum, sliced
100g shitake mushrooms
3 shallots, sliced
2 cloves garlic, diced
2 tsp ginger, finely chopped
1 bunch bok choy, chopped

Serves 4

METHOD

Soak noodles in water and drain. Season goanna pieces with salt and pepper spice mix. Heat wok, using a dash of oil stir-fry the noodles for 2 minutes. Remove from wok. Add the remainder of oil to wok. When hot add garlic, ginger and goanna pieces. Stir-fry until golden. Add remainder of ingredients and continue to cook for 1- 2 minutes. To serve place noodles on a paperbark plate if available and top with goanna stir-fry. Accompany this with a crisp white wine of your choice.

Roadside Wedgies

INGREDIENTS

1 wedge-tailed eagle breast cut into finger sized strips
1/2 cup flour
1/4 cup olive oil
1/2 tsp salt
2 tbs each of thyme and paprika
1 tbs cracked pepper
1/2 cup of Parmesan cheese

Serves whoever is hungry.

METHOD

Drive at least 50 km to heat up engine then stop and prepare breast strips. Lightly powder strips in flour. Combine oil and seasonings. Toss strips in seasoned oil until well coated. Lay flat on a baking sheet in a high-sided tray. Carefully balance tray on engine (secure if necessary). Close hood and drive for about another 50 - 100 km. Check under the hood and turn wedgies after 30 minutes. Sprinkle on Parmesan cheese and drive for another 20 minutes. Pull safely off the road to stop and serve with your choice of dipping sauce.

Chef's Tip
Suitable for quick roadside preparation - take a short drive then enjoy a hot, crispy snack.

Quoll au Vent

INGREDIENTS

400g quoll, roughly diced
4 large vol au vent pastry cases
4 cups vegetable stock
4 mushrooms, chopped
salt and pepper to taste
2 jars béchamel sauce
1 red chilli pepper, chopped
2 bunches asparagus, chopped
2 tbs light cream cheese

Serves 4

METHOD

Find somewhere to heat up pastry cases; a hot engine or tin roof will usually suffice. Broil quoll on the campfire in vegetable stock until cooked and beginning to fall apart. Remove from heat. When cool, shred meat into small pieces. Pour 1 jar of béchamel sauce into a large saucepan (use the second jar if more is needed later). Add meat, mushrooms, red chilli and asparagus, stirring over heat until asparagus softens. Add cheese. Continue stirring. Add salt and pepper to taste. Pour into pastry cases and bake for 15 minutes. Serve with salad.

Chef's Tip
Béchamel sauce is just a fancy name for white sauce.
That's why this is a gourmet cookbook.

The last specimen of eastern quoll recorded on mainland Australia was a female collected as roadkill near Sydney's Neilsen Park in 1963.
Australian Museum online database: www.amonline.net.au

Tasmanian Kidney Deville

INGREDIENTS

4 Tasmanian devil kidneys, halved
2 small mushrooms, sliced
8 grape tomatoes, halved
1 shallot, sliced
1 tsp plain flour
1 pinch cayenne pepper
1 pinch each, salt & pepper
2 tsp Black Devil Worcestershire sauce
1 tbs French mustard
1/4 cup dry white wine
fennel sprigs

Serves 2

METHOD

Skin and halve kidneys then remove core. Cut in half again, then toss pieces into flour seasoned with salt, pepper and cayenne pepper. Combine white wine, mustard and Black Devil sauce. Melt butter in frying pan and add seasoned kidneys. Fry for 4 minutes, turning often. Add tomatoes and mushrooms then cook for 1 minute over low heat. Pour in white wine mixture and simmer for 1 - 2 minutes then add shallots. Serve with a fried egg, toasted bread and garnish with fennel.

Chef's Tip
This dish makes an excellent and nutritious brunch after a hard night. So, why not try a little 'Hair of the Devil' and top it off with a delicious Tasmanian Pinot Noir.

A Species Truly on the Verge...

The Tasmanian devil presents a perfect example of roadkill exerting an unnecessary pressure on a species already threatened by habitat loss and disease.

As recently as the mid 1990's, Tasmanian devil population numbers were reported to be healthy, between 150,000 - 200,000 individuals. The appearance of Devil Facial Tumour Disease (DFTD) in 1996 and its subsequent spread has now put the Tasmanian devil high on the list of species under threat of extinction. Populations in some areas have been reduced by as much as 90%.

Understanding a little about animal behaviour can help. Tasmanian devils wean their young around mid to late summer. This is clearly a time when you can expect to see young and inexperienced devils on the roads. Watch out for them at night.

On May 21st 2008 under Tasmania's Threatened Species Protection Act 1995, the status of the Tasmanian devil was officially changed from vulnerable to endangered further highlighting its precarious future.

...the Tasmanian Devil

Efforts to manage DFTD include the 'Tasman Disease Suppression Trial' in southern Tasmania. The trial is an attempt to eradicate the disease from the Tasman peninsula's isolated wild population.

Approximately a quarter of Tasmanian devil deaths in this area were attributed to roadkill in 2006. The 'dusk to dawn' signage installed early in 2008 is designed to encourage drivers to slow down. The goal is to reduce roadkill as a contributing factor to local Tasmanian devil mortality.

Up to date research & information about the Tasmanian devil is available at: www.tassiedevil.com.au

WILDLIFE

45 km/h

DUSK TO DAWN

Reducing Roadkill

Some people say that the presence of roadkill reflects abundant local wildlife and hence is not a problem. However this does not mean that roadkill should be dismissed. Habitat loss, availability of roadside food & water, or the need to cross roads can artificially concentrate wildlife at the roadside. As animals die on the road, others move in to replace them, perhaps later becoming roadkill themselves.

Conservation issues aside, there are ethical matters to consider. Many animals struck by vehicles do not die immediately; they and their young may suffer unnecessarily from injury and starvation. Of course human injury is also a reason for concern, as is the negative experience of tourists seeing wildlife splattered all over the highway.

Road ecology researchers in Australia are striving to reduce the frequency of wildlife-vehicle collisions. Mitigation methods designed for use in North America and Europe (such as roadside reflectors, barriers and high frequency whistles) may not work here in Australia. Our expansive transportation networks and the diversity of wildlife mean that no single method is likely to be effective.

Fencing roadsides is not feasible for the nearly one million kilometres of road in Australia. Other strategies, such as roadside reflectors have been trialled with minimal effectiveness - cost considerations alone outweigh efficacy. Odour repellants, such as dog urine, have been trialled for kangaroos, but only work for some species, not others. There are claims that audible-warning devices attached to vehicles are an effective deterrent, despite there being no scientific evidence to support their effectiveness in relation to Australian wildlife.

Strategies that do work include alterations to the roadside. Wildlife roadkill tends to be clustered in 'hotspots' associated with factors such as steep verges (preventing escape from traffic), the presence of roadside water (popular in times of drought), or the need of wildlife to cross (feeding, breeding, migrating). Provision of appropriate roadside culverts, banks & cleared vegetation can reduce roadkill. Under- and overpasses have also been used effectively, allowing wildlife to cross under or to pass over roads. These methods are expensive, and best concentrated in known roadkill 'hotspots'.

Knowing that roadkill may be concentrated in certain areas allows specific targeting of prevention strategies. In addition to those above, perhaps the most effective method is that of changing human behaviours.

Australia's famous 'wildlife' roadsigns are familiar to us all. However signage highlighting local roadkill 'hotspots' can be of immense value. These signs have been used successfully in several places in Australia. Slowing down in these local areas or at certain times (such as from dusk to dawn) can reduce roadkill significantly. Such measures add only a few minutes to the total journey time.

The best method to help reduce roadkill is to take your time and enjoy the journey - getting there is half the fun.

Car Stickers

"Don't Squash Me" Tasmanian Conservation Trust, Tasmania
"Wildlife Zone Kangaroo Island" Wrong Side of the Road, South Australia

Mitigation measures for roadkill usually utilize one or a combination of the following:

- change animal behaviour (odour repellants, audible alarms) - species specific or ineffective
- change the roadside environment (fencing, roadside reflectors, underpasses and overpasses) - expensive
- change human behaviour (most amenable to change eg: road signs, speed limits, awareness via Roadkill Recipes)

Costs of Roadkill

Roadkill has economic, environmental and emotional costs. Animal suffering, biodiversity loss, distress to passengers and human injury are all costs to be considered. There are also the more tangible costs of vehicle repairs following a collision with an animal, or equally from swerving to avoid an animal and losing control of the vehicle.

Sadly roadkill is a part of 'modern' life in Australia, but it is also a source of wildlife mortality and road crashes that can be reduced.

"Three visitors from Victoria were conveyed to the Kangaroo Island General Hospital with minor injuries after the Nissan X-Trail they were in rolled over along the Playford Highway near Parndana. The accident happened when the driver swerved to avoid a lizard on the road. Damage to the vehicle is estimated at about $40,000."

'The Islander' Newspaper Kangaroo Island, 2004

The best defence is to

Slow Down and Watch Out for Wildlife.

The following is a flavour of wildlife roadsigns you may encounter on your Australian travels.

TREE KANGAROOS CROSSING NEXT 12 KM

AHEAD

NEXT 12 km

INJURED WILDLIFE 0500 540 000

AFTER

BEFORE

BANDICOOTS NEXT 5 km

HELP FOR WILDLIFE 0417–380687

CAUTION

NATIVE ANIMALS CROSSING OUR ROADS

CANE TOAD DETENTION CENTRE
LIVE TOADS ONLY, REMOVE TOADS FROM PLASTIC BAGS

We like our lizards frilled NOT grilled
BUSHFIRES COUNCIL N.T.
USH IRES COUNCIL N.T.

NEXT 88 km

MALLEE FOWL

NEXT 5 km

SPEEDING HAS KILLED CASSOWARIES

WILDLIFE

65 km/h

DUSK TO DAWN

BEWARE CASSOWARIES CROSS REGULARLY NEXT 2km

BIG LAGOON
Please Don't Kill Our Wild Animals DRIVE WITH CARE

The one paper in medical journals relating to kangaroo collisions in Australia supports the fact that most collisions occur:
- between 5pm & midnight
- in the countryside
- when drivers try to avoid a collision (40% direct collisions vs 60% rollover or collision with a secondary object such as a tree)

Abu-Zidan et al. (2002)

Safe Driving Tips

Wildlife-vehicle collisions are most likely to occur in the country, at night, and far from help. Rural Australia can be a lonely place to have a crash - finding help may be difficult as passing traffic is infrequent and mobile phones don't always work. Dedicated trauma services are usually located in capital cities, requiring evacuation by Royal Flying Doctor or State retrieval services. Many hours can pass before reaching definitive care.

Driving to the conditions will at least reduce the risk of a collision with wildlife, although not negate it entirely. The following tips are suggested:

Time your journey
Avoid travelling at times when wildlife are out and about. Many Australian native animals are nocturnal and data suggests most wildlife-vehicle collisions occur between 5pm and midnight. It is prudent to slow down around dusk and dawn, and also at night when visibility is reduced. Be wary of driving into the sun at dusk or dawn. Remember, some animals (particularly reptiles) tend to bask on bitumen during the day to warm up. Collisions with larger animals such as kangaroo, wombat, camel or stock may occur at any time.

Scan ahead & watch out for wildlife
Get your passengers to help scan the road ahead and warn if they see an animal or any other hazard. Drivers should be alert to changes ahead and in their peripheral vision.

Safe Driving Tips

Drive to the local conditions

Country speed limits are often 100km/h - this is a limit, not a challenge! Reduce your speed on dirt roads and where roadside verges are unsealed or densely vegetated. A kangaroo may lurk behind that tree! At night, drive such that you can safely stop within a third of the distance illuminated by your headlights. Reducing your speed gives both you and wildlife time to respond. Suggested speeds are a maximum 65 km/h on sealed and 40 km/h on unsealed roads when wildlife is prevalent.

Use high beams at night to illuminate the road

Consider dipping your lights if you do see wildlife - high beam may dazzle them and make animals more likely to run into the vehicle. Reduce speed if you see an animal, giving them both space and time whilst you pass slowly.

Maintain control

Avoid swerving, as this may cause loss of control and your vehicle may cross into oncoming traffic, rollover on the verge, or collide with a fixed object such as a tree. Brake safely, avoiding locking the wheels. If you are unable to stop, it may be safer to hit the animal rather than risk a crash through loss of control.

Don't drop rubbish

Food scraps may attract wildlife onto the roadside.

ROADKILL

The final leap is always the best;
a sudden burst of flame
whose ultimate brilliance
extinguishes itself.

Your landing leaves you
seemingly unblemished -
head on dusty pillow,
paws in fitful prayer -

but the heavens you sought
now pass on by
in the clouded mirror
of your eye.

Jill Gloyne
Kangaroo Island

What to do if you Hit an Animal

Despite all one's best efforts, sometimes collisions just happen – wildlife can be unpredictable, leaving you no chance to stop. Causing injury or death to an animal is distressing, and crashes in rural areas are compounded by distance from available help. The following is a brief guide in the event of a wildlife-vehicle collision.

Stop only where it is safe. Pull off the road, preferably on a straight section of road so that other road-users can see you (help avoid a further collision). Turn on your hazard lights and ensure the safety of yourself, your passengers and others. Remember to report any crash involving personal injury or property damage to Police (131444). In an emergency call 000.

Remove dead animals from the road. This helps to prevent carrion feeders also being hit, as well as clearing the road of carcasses that present a hazard – many drivers swerve into the oncoming lane to avoid driving over a dead animal.

If the animal is injured, treat it with respect and care. Animals that are hit require specialised care – either to be cared for and rehabilitated or to be humanely euthanased. Minimise stress by covering injured animals with a towel or blanket and then place them in a box or sack. Try not to disturb the animal by repeated viewing, nor to feed or give water to injured wildlife – wait until specialised help arrives.

USEFUL CONTACTS

Contact details for animal rescue groups vary from State to State, with no national contact number. However, you may be able to gain assistance from:

State Roadside Assistance 131 111
RSPCA 1300 ANIMAL
National Parks and Wildlife Service
Help For Wildlife 0417 380687 or www.helpforwildlife.com
State Animal Rescue Organizations

Before your trip think about what you might do in case of a problem or try and tap into local knowledge.

For example see www.helpforwildlife.com for excellent tips and advice.

– **WARMTH**
– **QUIET**
– **DARKNESS**
– **MINIMAL HANDLING**
– **NO FOOD OR WATER**
  UNLESS ADVISED BY A
  WILDLIFE CARER

HELP FOR WILDLIFE 0417–380687

43

Taphonomy - Laws of the Grave

Taphonomy is the study of what happens to a dead organism over time. It refers to all contributing physical, environmental and biological processes that have occurred from the moment of death. As such it is primarily used in the field of paleontology when seeking to understand the history behind fossilised remains.

Clearly the taphonomic time frame of roadkill is shorter than that of paleontological time, but the processes remain the same. Roadkill may be fresh, bloated, missing limbs, hard and crusty, mummified, a big pile of bones, or perhaps a small, very fertile patch of green on the roadside.

Which bones are left?

Why?

What has happened from the time of death to the moment when you begin to study the remains in front of you?

Forensics - Following the Clues

HOW? First and most importantly ask yourself what happened? Death is the final (though not necessarily immediate) result of impact with a moving vehicle. Was the animal hit, run over or perhaps both? Impact causes varying degrees of injury to the animal.

WHY? Was it the animal, the road, the driver or all of the above that caused the death? Why that species? Why here? Why this time of year? Only by asking questions can we begin to consider ways to reduce roadkill.

WHERE? What is the final resting place of the carcass? Did it die on the road, a result of hit and run? Was the animal dragged to the verge by a driver or perhaps by a scavenger? Did the animal crawl as far as it could before dying? Was it moved to its final resting place by weather conditions?

> Try a little forensic study of your own on the following photos...then later as you drive.

WHEN? The condition of the dead animal can help determine how long ago a death occurred. However the state of the carcass is subject to variables. The following are a few points that may help in trying to understand what happened and how long ago.

Road Surface: Is the road grey (warm) bitumen, unsealed red dust, ironstone or limestone? Remember speed is likely to be higher on bitumen.

Weather Conditions: Heat, cold, rain, humidity and damp all affect the rate of decomposition. In the colder, wet weather decomposition time is increased. In the dry summer heat mummification is not uncommon and hot weather can cause bloating.

Access by Scavengers: Scavengers, including invertebrates, are always present along the roadside. Not only will they consume flesh but carrion feeders can be responsible for removing limbs and scattering bones. Scavengers themselves are another clue to the mystery you are trying to solve - is this a primary or secondary incident? If you are looking at a carrion feeder is there another carcass nearby?

The Science of Decomposition-
Why Roadkill Smells So Bad

Claudius (King): *Where is Polonius?*

Hamlet: *In heaven; send thither to see: if your messenger find him not there, seek him i' the other place yourself. But, indeed, if you find him not within this month, you shall nose him as you go up the stairs into the lobby.*

From *Hamlet*, Act IV, Scene III

Hamlet's madness, whether it was real or imagined, left intact his sense of smell. As Hamlet infers, bacteria commence to break down body tissue and this produces the "stench of death". By-products from this bacterial decomposition include the aptly named cadaverine and putrescine. These organic amino acids are responsible for the stench of seasoned roadkill.

To put it bluntly, if roadkill is more than three hours old (less in hot weather), the process of decay will generate foul-smelling biogenic amines. These amines serve as an olfactory warning to potential human diners contemplating some of the recipes in this book. But remember that certain putrid odours, whilst repugnant to us,

prove irresistible to carrion feeders. Whether a particular odour is perceived as "bad" or "good" is in the nose of the beholder. In the case of humans, there is a certain innate adaptive advantage in associating foul-smelling food with illness and disease-causing microbes.

In Australia, carrion feeders such as goannas and Tasmanian Devils may be attracted to the road by the smell of decomposing flesh. Sadly there is no such thing as a free meal and many end up as victims of traffic themselves, aptly named "bystander" roadkill. Feral cats may suffer the same fate.

Wedge-tailed eagles and corvids are also scavengers that feed on roadkill – in this case, attraction is not by smell but by sight. These animals, in particular, the wedge-tailed eagle, also face the danger of becoming bystander roadkill as they feed – a good reason to remove roadkill from the road.

So remember – thanks to cadaverine and putrescine, if roadkill smells awful, it probably isn't safe to eat!

End of the Road

MUSIC FOR THE ROAD

Driving in the outback can be lonely and tedious. Whilst we are big believers in driving slowly and soaking up the surrounds, having music to listen to on long journeys can relieve the boredom.

So search the net, load up your MP3 player and try the following playlist for starters:

Roadkill Café (Bubba Mac Blues Band)
Squash that Bug (Brethren Fast)
Roadkill (Fig)
Splattered All Over the Highway (Kyf Brewer)
Roadkill Café (Mike Dekle)
Baby Kangaroo (Joe McDermott)
Dead Possum (Atomic Jefferson)
I Came Upon a Roadkill Deer (Bob Rivers)
Roadkill Café (Hillbilly Hellcats)
Shake Dem Bones (The Bellhops)
Squish Party (Jammy Man)
Roadkill (The Long Island Hornets)
Take a Penguin Out to Lunch (Animal Allstars)
Wallaby Stew (Denis Gibbons)

Earth, rock and river
Ants alert as chaos looms
Echidna is nigh

Brakes screech, no time lost
Distant dust and final breath
Lifeless…flattened spines

Further Reading

Australia has the unfortunate distinction of being the continent with the most mammalian extinctions in the past 200 years. This reflects mostly the effects of widespread habitat loss and the introduction of non-native species. Sadly roadkill is also a contributor, threatening some wildlife populations, as well as risking human and vehicle damage. Roadkill also presents an unsightly aspect of Australia to tourists and lovers of nature.

www.wrongsideoftheroad.com.au

The following references may be useful to interested readers.

Abu-Zidan, F., Parmar, K. & Rao S. (2002) Kangaroo-related motor vehicle collisions. J. Trauma 53 (2) : 360-363.

Bender, H. (2003) Deterrence of kangaroos from agricultural areas using ultrasonic frequencies: efficacy of a commercial device. Wildlife Society Bulletin 31 (4) : 1037-1046.

Dique, D.S., Thompson, J., Preece, H.J., Penfold, G.C., de Villiers, D.L. Leslie, R.S. (2003) Koala mortality on roads in south-east Queensland: the koala speed zone trial. Wildlife Research 30 : 419-426

Drennan F. (2007) Roadkill chef wins PETA award. Star of BBC3 Special Only Cooks With Accidental Motorway Meat. Accessed online at : http://www.wildmanwildfood.com/pages/peta2.html

Goosem, M., Bushnell S. & Weston N. (2006) Effectiveness of Rope Bridge Arboreal Overpasses and Faunal Underpasses in Providing Connectivity for Rainforest Fauna. In: ICOET 2005 304 - 316. Centre for Transport and the Environment, North Carolina, USA

Hobday, A. & Minstrell M. (2006) Speed kills: mitigating roadkill in Tasmania. Tasmanian Conservationist, Feb 2006 : 4-6.

Jones, M. (2000) Road upgrade, road mortality and remedial measures: impacts on a population of eastern quolls and Tasmanian devils. Wildlife Research 27 : 289-296.

Klocker, U., Croft, D. & Ramp D. (2006) Frequency and causes of kangaroo-vehicle collisions on an Australian outback highway. Wildlife Research 33 : 5-15.

Leeuwenburg, P. & Leeuwenburg, T. (2006) Roadkill recipes: a cookbook for visitors to Kangaroo Island. Publ. Jan 2006. ISBN 0 9758483 0 5

Magnus, Z., Kriwoken, L., Mooney, N. & Jones, M. (2004) Reducing the incidence of wildlife roadkill: improving the visitor experience in Tasmania. Technical Report CRC for Sustainable Tourism. ISBN 1 920704 79 5

Magnus Z. (2006) Wildlife roadkill mitigation information kit. A guide for local government and land managers. Sustainable Living Tasmania. Edited Chamberlain B. (2006)

Ramp, D. (2004) Sharing the environment: counting the cost of wildlife mortality on roads. National Wildlife Carers Conference, Conference proceedings, July 2004

Weir, E. (2002) Collisions with wildlife: the rising toll. CMAJ 166 : 775.

Zell, L. (2006) Australian Wildlife Roadkill. A wild discovery guide. Publ. November 2006. ISBN 0 9757184 3 6